11/13/14

HOW DOES VOICE RECOGNITION WORK?

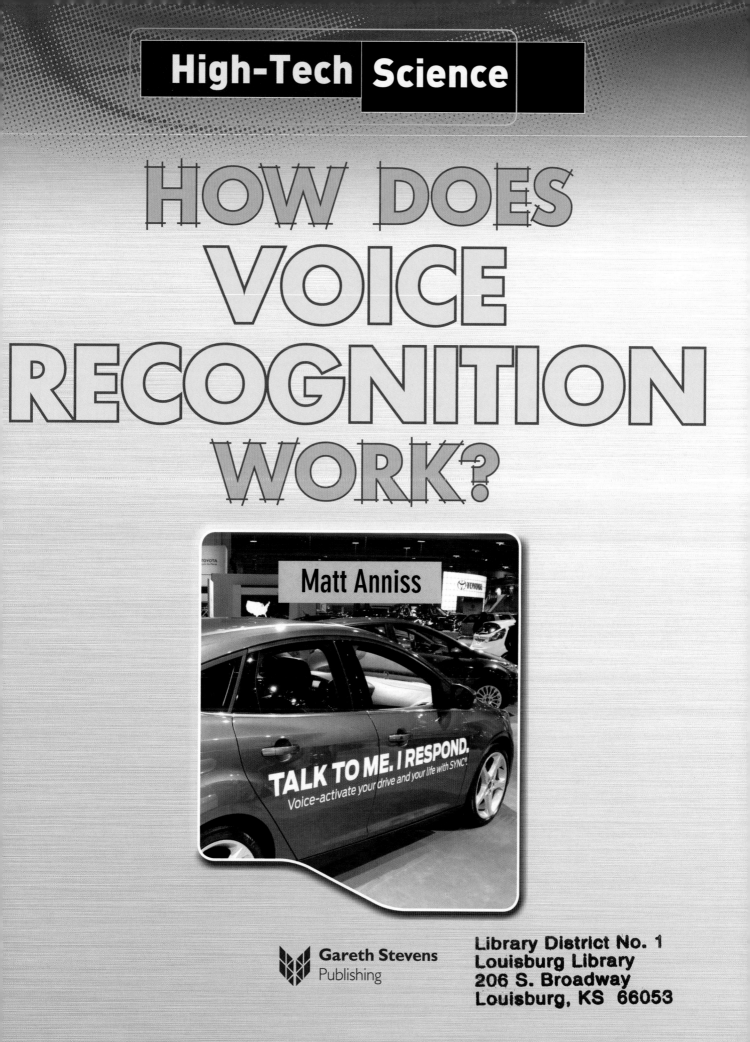

Matt Anniss

TALK TO ME. I RESPOND.
Voice-activate your drive and your life with SYNC®

Gareth Stevens
Publishing

Please visit our website, www.garethstevens.com. For a free color catalog of all our high-quality books, call toll free 1-800-542-2595 or fax 1-877-542-2596.

Library of Congress Cataloging-in-Publication Data

Anniss, Matt.
How does voice recognition work? / by Matt Anniss.
  p. cm. — (High-tech science)
Includes index.
ISBN 978-1-4824-0396-1 (pbk.)
ISBN 978-1-4824-0398-5 (6-pack)
ISBN 978-1-4824-0395-4 (library binding)
1. Identification — Juvenile literature. 2. Biometry — Juvenile literature. I. Anniss, Matt. II. Title.
QH323.5 A56 2014
599.94—dc23

First Edition

Published in 2014 by
Gareth Stevens Publishing
111 East 14th Street, Suite 349
New York, NY 10003

Produced by Calcium, www.calciumcreative.co.uk
Designed by Simon Borrough
Edited by Sarah Eason and Jennifer Sanderson

Photo credits: Cover: Shutterstock: Sergey Nivens. Inside: Dreamstime: Andresr 32, Czgur 34, Egomezta 44, Flashdevelop 42, Gillian08 40, Indigo 38, Jcjgphotography 22, Kalman89 37, Leighleo 36, Michaeljung 35, Monkeybusinessimages 28, MrFocus 8, Nobilior 31, Pcruciatti 43, Photojay 41, Ruigsantos 39, Shootalot 1, 45; Shutterstock: 5, 18, Aaron Amat 4, Andrey Popov 20, Anyaivanova 13, Auremar 21, Olga Besnard 29, Tomasz Bidermann 17, Bikeriderlondon 30, Joseph Calev 12, GG Pro Photo 26, Warren Goldswain 15b, Goodluz 18, 27, Geo Martinez 15t, Kubais 25, Monkey Business Images 3, 23, Sergey Nivens 7, Northfoto 24, Annette Shaff 33, Yuri Sheftsoff 9, Slpix 11, Leah-Anne Thompson 6, Viktorus 10, Lilyana Vynogradova 14; Wikimedia Commons: Gottscho-Schleisner, Inc. 16.

Printed in the United States of America

CPSIA compliance information: Batch #CW14GS. For further information contact Gareth Stevens, New York, New York at 1-800-542-2595.

CONTENTS

CHAPTER ONE
HOW DOES VOICE RECOGNITION WORK?

Voice recognition is one of the wonders of modern technology. Whether you want to buy movie tickets, find the answers to a question that has been bugging you, or even write a letter by simply saying it into a microphone, voice recognition technology is there to help.

Using voice recognition technology, we can book movie or theater tickets or check our bank balances on the telephone.

What Is Voice Recognition?

Voice recognition, sometimes known as speech recognition, has many different uses. However, the basic principles behind each application remain more or less the same. The user speaks into the voice recognition device, such as a microphone or telephone, and the computer in the device translates it to perform a specific task. This could be turning the words spoken into text, as if you were dictating a letter to somebody, opening a specific software application, such as Microsoft Word, or answering a question, as Apple's Siri program does on an iPhone.

Speak to Me

The applications of voice recognition technology are almost endless. Voice recognition systems can be used in people's homes or offices to turn light switches on and off. They can also be used to take credit card payments over the telephone. The systems can also assist people with disabilities in using their computers. Voice recognition is revolutionizing our lives and will continue to do so for many years to come.

SPEECH AND VOICE RECOGNITION

Some scientists argue that the term "voice recognition" should be used only to describe computer systems or applications that recognize and respond to a specific person's voice. They say that most voice recognition systems can respond to many different voices so they are actually "speech recognition" systems. For the purposes of this book, we will use both terms to describe the same thing—any technology that acts upon any spoken instructions.

Voice recognition software is sometimes used by journalists to quickly turn recordings of press conferences into written text.

SPEECH RECOGNITION BASICS

The technology behind speech recognition systems is quite complicated. However, it can be simplified if the basic principles behind the systems are broken down into smaller steps.

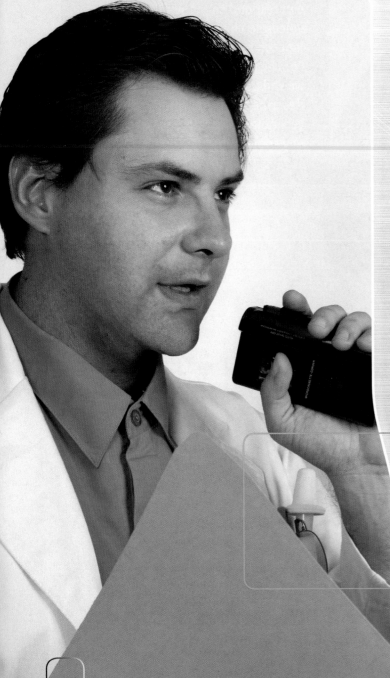

Speak Slowly

Whether you are calling an automated telephone service, such as the ones used by banks and companies that sell movie tickets, or using a speech recognition program on your computer, the technology behind the system is the same. First, the "user," or any person using the system, speaks into microphone. The microphone will in some way be connected to a computer. This could be a desktop PC, a computer inside a smartphone, or a laptop. It could also be a computer at the other end of a telephone line.

This man is speaking into the microphone of a personal voice recorder, or "dictaphone." This is the first stage of the voice recognition process.

When we speak, invisible waves of sound come out of our mouths. It is these waves that are picked up by microphones.

Computer Magic

While the user is speaking into the microphone, the voice recognition software will record the speech. This recording will then be turned into information that the computer can understand and analyze.

Analyzing and Acting

The process of recording and analyzing can take anything from a few hundredths of a second to a few seconds, depending on how quick the computer is. Once the computer has analyzed what has been said, it can act on the instructions. This could be performing simple tasks or turning words into text in a word processing document.

DIFFERENT NAMES FOR THE SAME TECHNOLOGY

Scientists and computer experts have many different names for speech recognition systems. Sometimes they are known as ASR (Automatic Speech Recognition) or STT (Speech To Text). Both names are used to refer to the same technology.

SPEECH TO DATA

Before the computer can act on any instructions, the voice recognition software inside the device must convert raw speech into information, or data, that the computer can understand.

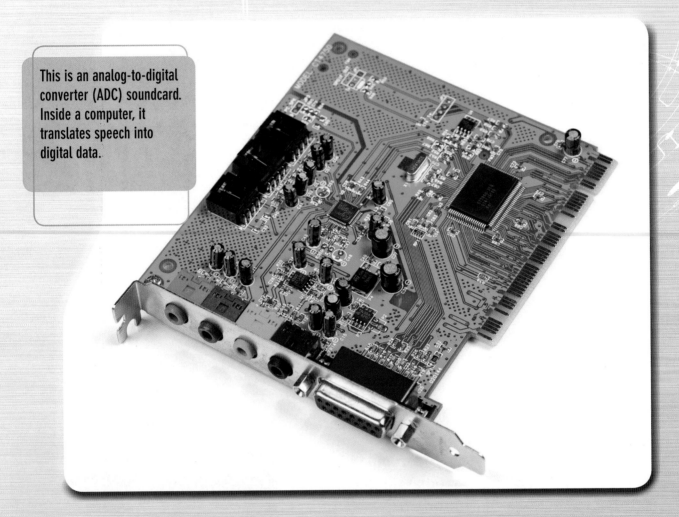

This is an analog-to-digital converter (ADC) soundcard. Inside a computer, it translates speech into digital data.

Good Vibrations

When people speak, they create vibrations in the air that can be heard as sounds. These vibrations are known as sound waves. When the sound waves are recorded, they are analog sound waves. Sound waves look like long, squiggly lines. If you use a music-making or movie-making program, such as Garageband or iMovie, you can see how sound waves look.

Computers cannot understand analog sound waves. Instead, they understand digital data, which is information recorded as a set of numbers. For speech recognition systems to work, the computers have to turn analog sound waves into digital data.

Analog to Digital

Speech recognition systems turn the sound waves into digital data using a device called an analog-to-digital converter (ADC). The ADC turns the sound into digital data by taking precise measurements of the wave at regular intervals—usually thousands of times a second. These measurements can then be turned into digital data. The digital data is analyzed using the system's speech recognition software.

SAMPLE MAGIC

The process of sampling, or digitizing, used by speech recognition systems is also used by music producers. They use sampling to record short segments of other people's music (usually from vinyl records or CDs), which they can then use to create a new song.

Your computer's ADC turns the words you speak into a microphone, such as the one on this hands-free headset, into digital data.

ANALYZING THE DATA

The process used by speech recognition systems to analyze the digital data converted from sound waves is incredibly complicated. It involves matching the data created with examples stored in the speech recognition software. The software must match the data to the digital representations of sounds, which are known as phonemes.

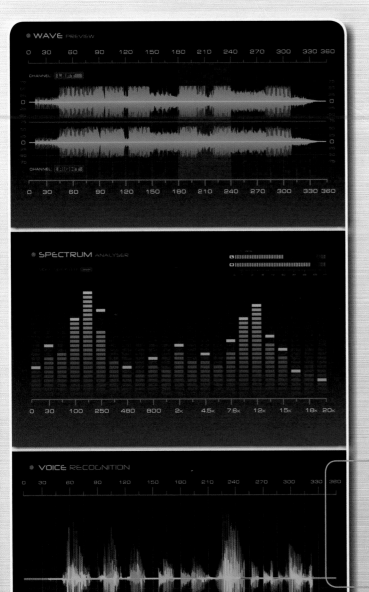

Building Blocks of Speech

Phonemes are the smallest element of a spoken language. They are the building blocks of speech. All words, when spoken, regardless of the language, are made up of a combination of different phonemes. To recreate or to understand what has been spoken, the speech recognition system must put these phonemes back together in the correct order.

When speech is recorded it is displayed on screen as sound waves. It is then turned into digital data.

Mix and Match

Putting the phonemes in the correct order to make meaningful words is a complex task. This is because many words use similar combinations of phonemes, or the words sound similar but mean different things. Today's speech recognition systems not only order these phonemes but they also have to try to match them with the words stored in the system's software.

To match the phonemes, scientists have invented a number of algorithms. These are computer processes based on complicated math. The algorithms help the system to examine each phoneme in context with any other phonemes around it. By doing this, the system can make an accurate guess as to exactly what was said.

PHONEME PHENOMENON

There are roughly 40 different phonemes in the English language. Some other languages, such as Mandarin and Japanese, have many, many more. Each phoneme represents a particular sound people use when speaking. Even a simple word such as "and" uses two phonemes: "ann" and "de." Try saying it out loud!

Phonemes are like the letters in a game of Scrabble. You need a number of phonemes to make a word.

ALGORITHMS

The complicated algorithms used by speech recognition systems figure out the probability that the sounds that have been identified are a specific word, phrase, or sentence.

The number of phonemes and words varies from language to language. For example, there are nearly twice as many words in English than in Spanish.

Problem Solving

There is a limited number of phonemes in the English language, and roughly 60,000 words in a basic English dictionary. Algorithms are used to sort through all the phonemes and words to accurately identify the words that were spoken by the user of the voice recognition device. To do this, scientists developed an algorithm called the hidden Markov model. It second-guesses the user and, using a detective-style process of deduction, figures out what was said.

It has taken scientists years of testing to perfect the technology behind today's voice recognition software.

Chain Reaction

In the hidden Markov model, each phoneme is treated like a link in a chain, with the completed chain making up a word. Each link is cross-referenced with the list of phonemes and words stored in the system's dictionary. To complete the chain, the system must figure out exactly which of the links comes next.

To help the system out, each likely link is given a "probability score," based on the possibility that it will come next (the higher the score, the more likely it is). By using this process of deduction, the algorithm will identify the right word more often than not.

MAKING A MARKOV

The hidden Markov model is named after a famous Russian mathematician named Andrey Markov, who lived from 1856 to 1922. The speech recognition algorithm that takes his name was developed only in the 1990s.

THE LIMITATIONS OF SPEECH RECOGNITION

Thanks to advances in algorithms, and more powerful home computers, speech recognition systems are much more accurate than they once were. However, there are still issues with many systems that scientists and software developers have yet to solve fully.

Too Noisy

Using the hidden Markov model guarantees quite accurate results most of the time. However, there are some flaws in it. If the user's microphone or telephone receiver picks up a lot of background noise—for example, if it is used in a busy office or at a train station—the system may struggle to accurately identify each individual sound.

This man will struggle to get his phone's voice recognition to work because there is too much noise at a train station.

Too Fast

Speech recognition systems also work better when people speak slowly and clearly. If you talk quickly and "run" words into each other (for example saying "y'all" instead of "you all"), the system will find it difficult to figure out what you are saying.

Voice recognition systems require slow, simple, and clear speech in order to work effectively.

THE NEED FOR SPEED

Today's voice recognition systems are capable of recording and sampling speech at very high speeds. Most telephone-based speech recognition systems now have a sample rate that allows them to record 8,000 samples each second!

People from different countries or regions within a country can have different accents, which make it difficult for voice recognition systems to work.

Slang and Accents

Speech recognition systems are also easily confused by slang words, as these may not appear in the dictionary. Regional accents can also be problematic. People in different parts of the same country often say the same things differently, and this can confuse speech recognition programs. This is why people often complain about automated telephone services that ask them to repeat words. The system does this because it cannot understand what was said.

CHAPTER TWO
VOICE RECOGNITION THROUGH TIME

Today's high-tech speech recognition systems began in the nineteenth century. During this time, it was discovered that sound waves could be converted into electrical signals. However, it was another 60 years before anybody attempted to turn sound into digital data.

Amazing Audrey

The big breakthrough in voice recognition came in 1952, when a company called Bell Laboratories successfully invented a computer that could recognize basic speech. The Automatic Digit Recognizer, or "Audrey" as it was known, was able to understand numbers (zero and one to nine). However, the speaker had to talk slowly and clearly, leaving large gaps between each number.

In the 1950s, the Bell Laboratories research center was home to the first basic speech recognition computer.

Moving So Fast

In the early 1970s speech recognition technology really began to move forward. Several systems were invented that understood a greater number of words as well as numbers. However, as the computers of the 1970s were not very powerful or advanced, the speech recognition systems were of limited use.

IBM's "Shoebox" voice recognition computer was the first machine to recognize both words and numbers.

Government Help

The US government saw the potential of speech recognition, though, and in early 1971 it began to invest money into the Department of Defense's DAPRA Speech Understanding Research (SUR) program. This ran for 5 years and managed to develop a system called "Harpy" that understood 1,011 words—roughly the same as an average 3-year-old. As a result of this research, speech recognition systems were on sale by the late 1970s. They were not cheap, though, and the best system could cost $100,000!

THE SUPER SHOEBOX

In 1962, US computer company IBM developed a computer that not only recognized speech, but could also perform basic math. The "Shoebox," as it became known, recognized numbers from zero to 10, as well as commands such as "plus," "minus," and "total."

PROBLEM SOLVING

Early voice recognition systems were proven to work but they were limited in what they could do. They could recognize only a limited number of words and they were based on known rules of the English language, such as grammar. For the systems to work, words and sentences had to be spoken slowly and they had to abide by the rules.

Big Step Forward

The invention of the hidden Markov model algorithm in the early 1980s (see page 13) changed speech recognition systems forever. Invented by two computer programmers, Jim Baker and Fred Jelinek, the hidden Markov model split words into phonemes. This revolutionized speech recognition by considering the probability that certain sequences of sounds made up specific words.

Voice recognition first became popular as a system for recording what was said between lawyers and witnesses in courtrooms.

Health care professionals were some of the first people to use voice recognition in their everyday working lives.

On Sale Now

During the 1980s, expensive speech recognition systems were sold to companies for use in the health care and legal professions. While advanced for the time, they were nowhere near as advanced as the systems we know and use today. One of the systems' biggest drawbacks was the computers used at the time. These were slow, basic, and expensive. At this time, few people owned home computers, and the systems were unsuitable for them anyway.

CHILD'S PLAY

The first mass-market use of speech recognition technology was not computer software. It was, in fact, a pioneering children's doll named Julie. Launched in 1987, Julie featured speech recognition technology that allowed users to teach her words. Julie also responded to questions. She even giggled out loud if you tickled her!

VOICE RECOGNITION COMES OF AGE

During the 1990s, faster, cheaper computers and better-quality voice recognition systems combined to bring speech recognition software to the home. The move toward making it part of our everyday lives had begun.

Jim Baker's Dragon software led a revolution in voice recognition by making the software cheap enough to appeal to office managers.

Dragon Dictate

In 1990, one of the scientists behind the hidden Markov model, Jim Baker, launched a new voice recognition system—Dragon Dictate. Dragon Dictate was the first speech recognition system aimed at home computer users. However, at $9,000 it was still too expensive for most people to afford.

Naturally Speaking

Baker spent the next 7 years perfecting his system. In 1997, he replaced it with a new system called Dragon NaturallySpeaking. Costing around $700, this had suddenly made voice recognition software much more affordable. The system recognized continuous speech and featured a dictionary of around 10,000 words. Users could speak naturally, at around 100 words a minute, and it would keep up. However, users had to spend 45 minutes "training" it to understand them.

On the Line

The 1990s saw the development of another great speech recognition system that is widely used today. The automated telephone system uses speech recognition technology in a different way. Users dial a number and a recorded voice on the other end of the line asks a series of questions. The system recognizes the answers and reacts accordingly.

MEET VAL

The first ever "dial-in interactive voice recognition system," or automated telephone service, was launched in 1996. It was based on a system called VAL, which was capable of listening to what you said, understanding different options, and giving you information based on your answers to simple questions.

Today's automated telephone systems have their roots in BellSouth's pioneering VAL system of 1996.

VOICE RECOGNITION FOR EVERYONE

Since the turn of the century, voice recognition technology has really advanced. Today, what was once incredibly expensive software is available to everyone. There are voice recognition systems built into smartphones, laptops, and home computers to make this technology a part of our everyday lives.

In the Computer

As computer speech recognition programs have become more accurate and faster and people's home computers have become more powerful, computer manufacturers have started building speech recognition software into their systems.

Since 2005, Microsoft and Apple Computers have included speech recognition and voice commands in their operating systems. Operating systems, such as Windows and Mac OS, are the framework around which all home computers are built. Using speech recognition means that people can tell their computers what to do—for example, opening and closing activity windows or connecting to the Internet.

What can I help you with?

Siri, the iPhone's "digital assistant," recognizes what you say, acts upon instructions, and answers questions.

It is now possible to make calls, send emails, and navigate menus on your cell phone using voice commands.

GOOGLE VOICE

In 2008, the Google search engine allowed users to do an Internet search by speaking into their computer or cell phone instead of keying in the information. This system, called Google Voice Search, soon became so popular that, in 2011, it was turned into a smartphone app.

On the Phone

The development of smartphones, such as Apple's iPhone, brought about the next big advance in speech recognition technology. Today, all smartphones come bundled with software programs based on voice recognition technology. The most famous of these is the iPhone's "Siri" program, which will try to answer almost any question, often with very funny results!

CHAPTER THREE

VOICE RECOGNITION SYSTEMS TODAY

There are two main types of voice recognition system used today: those designed for a large number of users and those meant to be used by only one or two people. Each system has different strengths and weaknesses, and each is used for a specific purpose.

Banks often use automated telephone systems to deal with simple customer questions, such as how much money is in an account.

Many Users

The most popular speech recognition systems are those designed for use by a large number of people. These are the systems used by automated telephone services and apps, such as Google Voice Search. For this kind of voice system to work properly, it has to be set up to recognize only a few common words and commands. However, these systems can recognize different accents and speech patterns.

The companies that operate automated voice recognition systems decide the words, commands, and numbers it will recognize, based on the nature of their business. They then train the system to recognize the many different ways people from different areas say these words, commands, and numbers. By doing this, the system should be able to cope with different regional or national accents.

Say It Again

When you call an automated telephone service, such as one used to book movie or concert tickets, it sometimes has difficulty understanding or recognizing what you say. If this is the case, a voice may ask you to repeat what you have said. This type of system is no use to those who want to speak a lot, as it really only understands numbers and very basic words, such as "yes," "no," and names of places or popular movies.

Supercomputers, such as these, are needed to run big automated telephone services that deal with thousands of calls per minute.

LIMITED USERS

The second type of voice recognition system is designed for use by a very limited number of users, perhaps just one or two people. It is this type of system that experts have been perfecting since the 1980s.

Very Accurate

Limited user voice recognition systems are far more accurate than the systems used in automated telephone services. Typically they can get between 85 and 90 percent of words right. They are also able to recognize many more words—usually up to 60,000. One of the most well-known programs that uses this kind of system is Dragon NaturallySpeaking, the pioneering speech recognition program, which was developed in the 1990s (see page 20).

To get the best out of your voice recognition software, you must use a microphone to train it to understand the way you speak.

If more than one person is using a speech recognition software, each person must spend around 45 minutes training the system.

Training the System

As their name suggests, limited user systems work well if they are used by a very small number of people. This is because they become familiar with the way these people speak and pronounce particular words. However, there is a catch to using these systems—for them to perform well, each user must spend some time training the software to recognize their speech patterns.

TESTING THE SYSTEM

Training a speech recognition system on your computer is surprisingly easy. After a quick microphone test, the system will then ask you to read out a short passage of text displayed on your computer screen. This is so that it can begin to learn your speech patterns and how you say certain key words.

CHAPTER FOUR

VOICE RECOGNITION SYSTEMS IN ACTION

Today, voice recognition technology has many different uses. Some of these uses we encounter in our daily lives, but there are many other applications of voice recognition that you are probably not aware of.

Telephone Services

Speech recognition in automated telephone services is becoming increasingly common. Today, these systems are used mostly by companies that have call centers and have to deal with many people on a daily basis. These organizations include banks and cable television operators as well as box offices and electricity companies.

Utilities companies often use automated services to allow families to tell them their new address if they are moving.

Saving Money

Although these systems are expensive to buy and set up, in the long run the companies save money. They do not have to employ as many people to answer their phones. They can also use the system to direct each call to the right department. This is done using a set of prerecorded questions, the answers to which will help the system forward the call on to the correct part of the organization.

Automated services would prove impossible at tourist attractions such as the Eiffel Tower because of the number of accents and speech patterns that would need to be programmed into the system.

CALL FAILURE

Automated telephone services that use speech recognition do not have a good reputation. Many people find them very annoying, as they seem to fail regularly. When this happens, it is often because the system does not understand what the person has said. People with strong regional accents or foreigners have the most problems with these systems.

Speak After the Tone

Automated telephone services are also good for companies who have a lot of customers and deal with sensitive information, such as banks. These companies can use the automated service to identify the caller, asking for passwords and other key details, before allowing the customer to speak to a representative. However, not all automated telephone systems use speech recognition. Some ask people to use their phone's keypad to type in numbers instead.

AT WORK

Speech recognition technology has transformed the working world. Today, many people use speech recognition systems in their workplace, and in some areas it is becoming as essential as a telephone and computer.

Saving Time

When speech recognition technology first became popular during the late 1990s and early 2000s, makers of voice recognition software aimed their products at businesses. Today, many companies run systems aimed at limited users. Instead of dictating letters to a secretary or assistant who would write them down, many managers now choose to dictate their letters and reports into a computer running speech recognition software. The software turns their spoken words into text, so they can write and send letters quickly.

Speech recognition has changed the traditional role of the secretary forever. Today, businesspeople dictate notes and letters into their computers.

Doctors currently have a choice between two voice recognition systems: front end and back end speech recognition. Front end systems display the words, as you say them, onto a computer screen. Back end systems, on the other hand, analyze previously made recordings and email the analyzed document to the doctor a few hours later.

Popular Systems

Using speech recognition software to dictate notes and letters has become a popular way of working across a range of industries, but is arguably most popular in the legal and health care professions. It saves lawyers, attorneys, and doctors valuable time. Speech recognition options built into computer operating systems have also become increasingly popular with those who struggle to type. Using voice commands, they can control their computers without having to touch the mouse, trackpad, or keyboard.

Voice recognition systems have helped reduce the amount of paperwork doctors and nurses need to complete every day.

ON THE MOVE

Today, many of us carry around tiny speech recognition systems in our pockets. Thanks to the integration of voice commands into the operating systems of smartphones, you can now use these phones without ever touching the screen or keypad.

You can use voice commands on your cell phone to select and play music.

In Command

There are three popular operating systems used in today's smartphones. They are Google's Android, Microsoft's Windows Phone, and Apple's iOS. All three of these operating systems respond to voice commands. They all work in a similar way, too.

Normally, you have to hold down a button (or in the case of Android phones, access the Google Voice app). You then need to tell your phone what to do by saying commands, such as "phone mom," or "search the Internet." You can even ask your phone to search nearby for places to eat, or play a particular song or album.

Apple's Siri software on the iPhone is one of a number of speech recognition systems built in to today's smartphones.

Siri

Use your voice to send messages, set reminders, search for information, and more.

Digital Assistant

The speech recognition system built into iPhones is called Siri. Siri is at the cutting edge of speech recognition technology. Not only does it respond to simple commands, but it also learns about you by remembering what you search for on the Internet and what music you listen to. It cross-references the way you speak with a huge bank of accents and speech patterns stored in its memory. The more you use Siri, the better it understands you.

SIRI

Apple's voice recognition system, Siri, is quite revolutionary. It does not just respond to simple commands, such as "play music," but it will also try to answer simple questions, speak back to you, and, if you ask silly questions, give you silly answers!

TRAINING

Speech recognition systems are widely used in the workplace in many different ways. One very important way is in the training of people to do difficult and demanding jobs.

In Control

Air traffic controllers have one of the most difficult and stressful jobs. It is their responsibility to ensure that planes not only take off and land safely at airports, but that they also take the correct route through the skies. Training new air traffic controllers takes a lot of time and is very difficult. In the past, it required a lot of input from experienced controllers, who would test out their recruits' skills by pretending to be a pilot trying to land a plane.

Before they begin work, junior air traffic controllers test their skills against a computer loaded with special voice recognition software.

Simulation

Today, experienced air traffic controllers no longer have to train the junior controllers in the same way. Instead, a trainee air traffic controller goes into a simulation booth and is given a specific task to perform, such as safely guiding a plane into an airport. In a real-life situation, the controller would speak to a pilot. In this training situation, there is no pilot—just a computer loaded with prerecorded speech and a voice recognition system. The computerized pilot responds to what the trainee controller says. Air traffic controllers are supposed to use only about 150 standard phrases when talking to pilots. However, the leading training systems recognize more than 500,000 different phrases.

Learning Mandarin can be made easier using voice recognition software. Programs have been designed for people to learn foreign languages.

HELP FOR LEARNERS

Speech recognition systems are now being used to help people learn foreign languages. Many popular computer assisted language learning (CALL) programs include speech recognition technology to help people learn to say certain words more clearly.

FLYING HIGH

Ever since the US Department of Defense invested huge amounts of money in research into speech recognition in the 1970s, the military has seen the potential in voice commands and controls.

Help for Pilots

Over the last few years, air forces around the world have started to experiment with using voice recognition systems in fighter jets. It makes a lot of sense, as fighter pilots have a lot to do in combat. They must fly a plane at high speed and at the same time, they must communicate with their commanders and, sometimes, fire missiles.

HELICOPTER COMMAND

The US Air Force is investing a lot of money in creating a voice recognition system that can be used inside the cockpits of attack helicopters. This is a great development in voice recognition because noise can reduce the effectiveness of voice control systems, and a helicopter cockpit is incredibly noisy.

If the US Air Force manages to create voice recognition software that works inside helicopters, it will allow pilots to concentrate solely on flying.

F-16s

A number of F-16 fighter jets that are used by the US Air Force now use speech recognition voice control systems. Pilots can use the system to set radio frequencies, turn on the autopilot system, set steering controls, and change the information displayed on the screens in the flight deck.

Eurofighters

Other air forces around the world have also developed speech recognition systems in some of their planes. The Eurofighter jet, which is used by the British Royal Air Force (RAF), has a system that requires each pilot to create his or her own "template." This template helps the pilot to train the plane's system to understand how the pilot speaks. The RAF says that training and using the system this way has helped lighten the load of pilots, allowing them to concentrate on flying their planes.

Flying an attack jet is very complicated but slightly easier now thanks to revolutionary voice command systems for pilots.

ROBOTS

It might sound like something from a science fiction movie, but scientists have recently invented robots with human characteristics—including the ability to recognize and respond to different voices.

Meet ASIMO

In 2000, Japanese company Honda unveiled the most humanlike robot yet: ASIMO (short for Advanced Step in Innovative Mobility). Now featured at an attraction at Disneyland, ASIMO walks and moves like a person. More amazingly, ASIMO can recognize faces, move out of the way when somebody approaches, and carry out tasks such as moving objects. He can even run, albeit slowly.

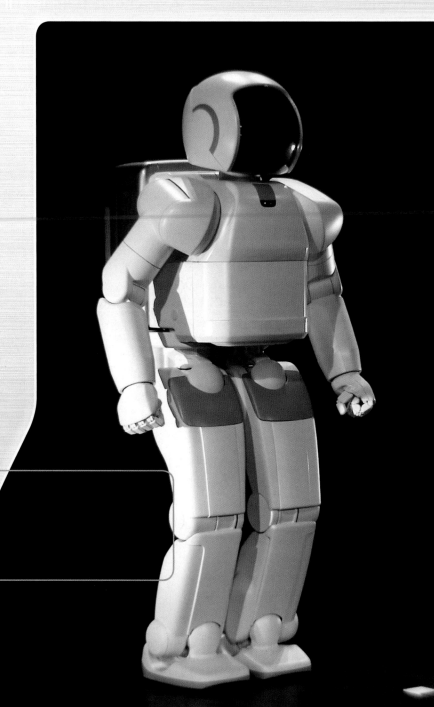

The ASIMO robot is the result of nearly 20 years of research in Honda's laboratories.

ASIMO Knows You

Honda's ASIMO has built-in speech recognition technology. This means that he can respond to voice commands. He will turn his head toward the direction of the person speaking to him (or an unusual sound, such as breaking glass or a heavy object hitting the ground), and he can even respond to simple questions. Many speech recognition systems can recognize a few different voices, but few act on it. ASIMO is different because he can recognize 10 different voices and respond accordingly. As well as recognizing voices, he also learns names. This means that when you talk to him, he will address you by your name, like he knows you!

Drivers can use Ford SYNC to change some of the car's controls using voice commands.

THE TALKING CAR

Many of the latest cars feature speech recognition technology. Products such as Ford SYNC, found in some of Ford's cars, allow drivers to make phone calls, play music, and control the satellite navigation system. In the future, car manufacturers hope to create systems that respond to commands and also talk back.

CHAPTER FIVE

THE FUTURE OF VOICE RECOGNITION

Voice recognition technology has advanced a great deal in the last 25 years. Given the speed of these developments, it is likely that new speech recognition technology will be even more sophisticated in coming years. So what can we expect from voice recognition technology in the future?

A universal translator will make conversations between people who speak different languages much easier.

WAR TALK

During the Iraq war, the US Army developed a two-way translator called TRANSTAC. TRANSTAC used speech recognition to understand both Arabic and English. It was able to translate from one language into the other, which proved vital to soldiers based in Iraq.

The Universal Translator

There are many skilled translators in the world. These people specialize in translating from one language into another. Most professional translators know about four or five languages. However, experts say that there are around 6,500 different languages spoken in the world today. Imagine being able to carry around a small, computerized device that is able to understand any one of these languages, and translate it into your chosen language. Scientists think that one day, voice recognition technology will make this possible. In fact, research has already begun to create what scientists call the "universal translator." To create a device that could instantly translate between all those different languages will take computer scientists many years.

Some Success

The universal translator may still be a dream, but there are products available that can instantly translate between different spoken languages. SpeechGear's "Compadre Interact" software is not a universal translator, but it recognizes 41 different languages. If you speak into it, it can instantly translate and play back your words in any of those languages. It allows people to hold conversations even if they do not speak the same language.

ARTIFICIAL INTELLIGENCE

Although the universal translator is still some way off from becoming an everyday device, it is not the only avenue being explored by scientists and software engineers. They think that in the future, there will be many other uses for voice recognition technology.

The Home of the Future

Computer scientists believe that one day, our homes could come with speech recognition technology built into different parts of the house. It is already possible to have light switches that respond to voice commands. In the future, you may be able to lock and unlock your doors and windows using your own voice. These voice command systems could also double as security systems by responding only to the speech patterns and exact sound of a specific speaker.

One day, robots might not just recognize human speech, but also truly understand it. This is what is known as artificial intelligence.

The US government has spent millions of dollars trying to create software that can translate foreign language news broadcasts in a matter of seconds.

Artificial Intelligence

Some computer scientists also believe that speech recognition will play a key role in developing computers, robots, and other devices with true artificial intelligence. At present most speech recognition systems can recognize words, phrases, and speech patterns, and act on them. However, the systems still do not understand what the user is saying.

A device or computer with true artificial intelligence would actually understand everything you say. They will be able to think for themselves, just like people do. Although it sounds far-fetched, it is thought that the technology may be available within 25 years.

NEWS TRANSLATOR

Since the mid-2000s, the US government has funded a project called GALE (Global Autonomous Language Exploitation). The scientists on the project are developing systems that monitor broadcasts in Mandarin and Arabic, before translating them into English. The scientists behind GALE hope that in the future, they will be able to do the same with many different languages.

YOU ARE IN CONTROL

Voice recognition systems have come a long way in a short space of time. They have developed from simple computers that understand a few numbers to amazing devices capable of translating between many different languages. In the process, they have changed our lives forever.

In the future, our lives could be like the *Star Trek* movies, where every piece of technology responds to voice commands.

From Sci-Fi to Real Life

Only recently television viewers and movie audiences marveled at the speech recognition systems imagined by the writers of *Star Trek*. Now, similar systems are part of our everyday lives. Consider your own life. You or someone in your house may own a smartphone that can be controlled using voice commands. You may have used an automated telephone service built around speech recognition technology. Someone you know may even own a Ford car that uses the SYNC system.

Early Days

With all of these amazing uses of speech recognition systems around us, it is important to remind ourselves that the technology is still in its early stages. It is still far from perfect, as anyone who has used an automated telephone system will tell you. However, most voice recognition systems still manage to understand between 85 and 97 percent of words and phrases. Thirty years ago, they managed less than 50 percent. How many years will it take to get to 100 percent?

WHERE TO NEXT?

We can all imagine how speech recognition will change our lives in the future, from toilets that flush on command, and earphones that instantly translate foreign languages, to cars that drive themselves and robots that talk back to us. What do you think the future holds for voice recognition technology?

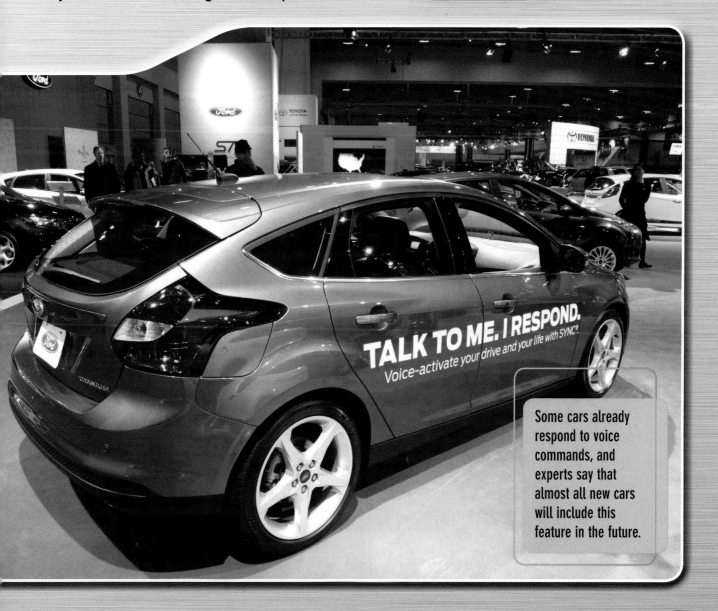

TALK TO ME. I RESPOND.
Voice-activate your drive and your life with SYNC®

Some cars already respond to voice commands, and experts say that almost all new cars will include this feature in the future.

GLOSSARY

algorithms a set of rules for solving a problem in a set number of steps

analog the opposite of digital. Sound waves are analog.

artificial intelligence the ability of a machine to think and understand things like a human being does

automated designed to run with minimal human control, for example, automated telephone services

call centers offices where many operators man phones so that a company can deal with a large number of calls from customers

data information

digital based on numbers

digital data information in a form that can be understood by digital devices such as computers

digitizing the process of turning sound, pictures, or movies into a digital file on a computer

operating system the software included in computers, smartphones, and tablet computers that makes them work

phonemes the distinctive sounds that make up spoken language

phrase a sequence of two or more words that is not a fully formed sentence

probability how likely or possible it is that something happens

regional accents differences in the way people speak according to where they live or were brought up. Accents are why people from New York sound different from those who come from Texas.

research studying something and conducting experiments in order to learn more about it

sampling the process of recording and analyzing sounds

science fiction (sci-fi) a style of book, movie, or television series inspired by future technology and the wider universe

software an application on a computer designed for a specific purpose, for example, browsing the Internet or speech recognition

software engineer a scientist who writes or develops computer software programs

sound waves the vibrations created in the air by sounds

speech patterns unique variations in the way different people speak, for example how quickly they talk, how they say certain words, and whether they have a regional accent

translation changing spoken or written words from one language into another

translator someone or something capable of translating spoken or written words from one language to another

word processing describes computer programs, such as Microsoft Word, that allow users to write documents

FOR MORE INFORMATION

Books

Goldsmith, Mike, and Tom Jackson. *Computer (Eyewitness)*. New York, NY: Dorling Kindersley, 2011.

Sutherland, Adam. *The Story of Apple*. New York, NY: Rosen Central, 2012.

Websites

Watch videos of Honda's amazing robot, ASIMO, in action at:
http://world.honda.com/ASIMO

For a good explanation of how voice recognition works, go to:
www.ehow.com/how-does_4895460_voice-recognition-work.html

Find out exactly how Apple's famous "digital assistant" works at:
http://electronics.howstuffworks.com/gadgets/high-tech-gadgets/siri.htm

You can try using voice commands and speech recognition on your home PC using this simple guide at:
http://windows.microsoft.com/en-us/windows-8/using-speech-recognition

INDEX